For
Warren, my rock (star).

There was music in the air
It sounded like it was in the house
It turned out to be a voice somewhere
That was singing VERY LOUD

It was a horrible sounding noise at that
Simple enough, and sung without fear

The words were easy to understand
It's just that the song was so hard to hear

...A LOUD and ANNOYING sort of tune
with its "music" filling all of the rooms

With a song in her heart she tried to sing
But sweet little Sophie couldn't sing a thing!

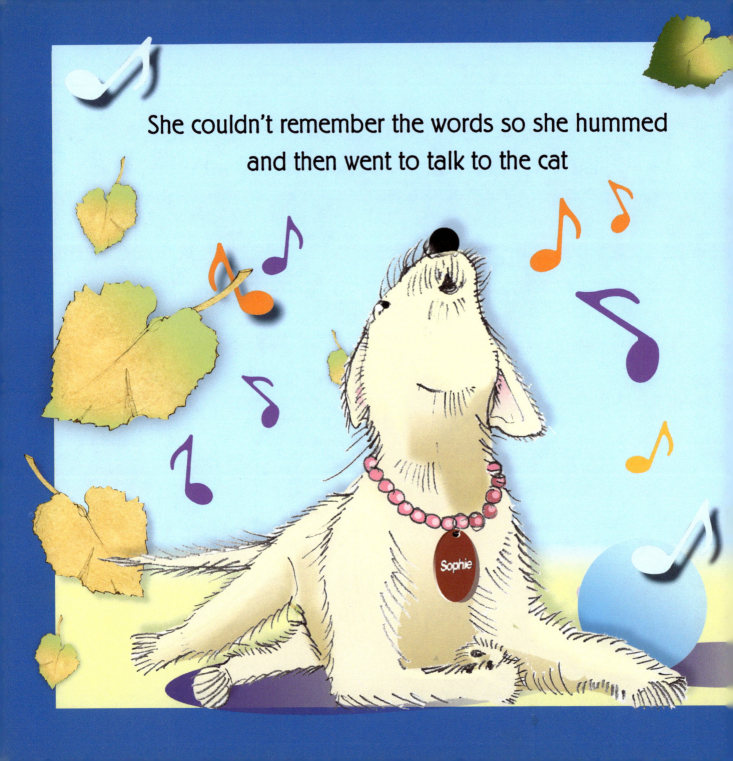

She couldn't remember the words so she hummed
and then went to talk to the cat

After he sat down and then heard her sing
He informed our dear Soph she was flat!

...and that - was - that.

She talked to the birds about their beautiful songs
She wanted to find out where she had gone wrong

She needed to practice at least every day
But everyone told her to please go away!

At the end of the day what really does matter
(as Sophie kept getting flatter and flatter)

...is to go on ahead
and push through your fears
Just tell everyone else to
"Please hold your ears!"

GOOD NIGHT.

ABOUT THE AUTHOR | ILLUSTRATOR

With a focus on graphic design, Jamison has been working for over 30+ years in Los Angeles, CA and Monterey County, CA, winning community as well as international awards for her design and illustration.

With this series of books being published and collected throughout the world, *Sophie!* stories will capture your heart as you read aloud the adventures of a small dog having a big life with her friends. Big triumphs abound in these small books, and life's lessons are learned with patience, support and care. As an illustrator Jamison creates a style of simplistic spare realism – and the poems are constructed to be easy and 'visual'.

Jamison studied graphic design and illustration at the Art Center College of Design, Pasadena, CA and looks at lots and lots of talented artists in the children's section of the local library, as well as life at "Tiny Ranch" for inspiration. The animals provide an endless supply of entertainment and ideas!

Jamison lives in Monterey, CA with her fabulous husband Warren and a small herd of dogs and cats. Sophie and her pals in the book are real. The cats rule.

JK PUBLISHING
jamisonk.com
2018

Copyright ©2018 Jamison Kaufman
All rights reserved.
ISBN: 978-0-692-08985-9
Published by jamisonk.com | publishing

CPSIA information can be obtained
at www.ICGtesting.com
Printed in the USA
LVHW07n2226200318
570539LV00003B/3/P